DODGE PICKUPS
1939-1978
Photo Album

Edited with introduction by
Don Bunn

Iconografix
Photo Album Series

Iconografix seeks collections of archival photographs for reproduction in future books. We require a minimum of 120 photographs per subject in our Photo Archive Series and Photo Album Series, and a minimum of 500 photographs per subject in our Photo Gallery Series. We prefer subjects narrow in focus, i.e., a specific model, or manufacturer, railroad, racing venue, etc. Photographs must be of high-quality, suited to reproduction in an 8x10-inch format. We willingly pay for the use of photographs.

If you own or know of such a collection, please contact: The Publisher, Iconografix, PO Box 446, Hudson, Wisconsin 54016 USA.

Iconografix
PO Box 446
Hudson, Wisconsin 54016 USA

Text Copyright © 1998

Iconografix books are offered at a discount when sold in quantity for promotional use. Businesses or organizations seeking details should write to the Marketing Department, Iconografix, at the above address.

Library of Congress Card Number 97-075277

ISBN 1-882256-82-4

98 99 00 01 02 03 04 5 4 3 2 1

Printed in the United States of America

Dodge's V-Series trucks for 1939 were utterly new. Shown is a VC half-ton pickup.

INTRODUCTION

In the world of pickups the two most overworked adjectives are tough and rugged. These words describe the pickups Dodge built from 1939 to 1978, but the adjective which comes to my mind when talking about Dodge pickups is "practical". After all, the purpose of a truck is to move the greatest weight in the shortest time, at the least cost. Practical is the best word to describe the pickups Dodge engineers designed to fulfill the purpose of a truck.

Our Photo Album begins with the year 1939. That year Dodge engineers took a clean sheet of paper to engineer and style a line of out-and-out new pickups. These pickups were the first in the "modern" era for they were a complete break from those which preceded. Pickup styling became more truck-like in appearance than had been the norm up to 1939. Starting with 1939's pickups we may legitimately use our two favorite pickup adjectives—tough and rugged. But beyond that these pickups were designed and engineered to better fulfill the purpose of a truck, that is for their load carrying ability, economy and durability. As almost a contradiction to the above, in 1939 engineers still rated a half-ton pickup for a 1,000 lb. payload, a three-quarter-ton pickup for a 1,500 lb. payload and a one-ton pickup for a 2,000 lb. payload. As a practical matter, however, owners consistently exceeded manufacturer's specifications.

Dodge pickups built between 1939 and 1947 are called Job-Rated Era trucks. Job-Rated Era pickups continued until 1947 with only minor styling and engineering changes and improvements. In the middle of this era, production of civilian trucks was suspended in order to concentrate on building approximately 450,000 4WD three-quarter and one-and-one-half-ton military trucks for WWII.

Job-Rated trucks gave way to a reengineered and restyled line of Pilot-House Era pickups in 1948, which continued through the 1953 model year. Some of the highlights of Pilot-House Era pickups included the industry's deepest cargo box (meaning the greatest carrying capacity), a set-back front axle for better handling, greater payloads and a shorter turning radius. Other highlights included a chair height seat, excellent visibility through increased glass area and the widest cab in the industry. A subtle, modern styling touch was integral cab-wide front fenders, in place of the former bolted on type.

The Dodge reputation for practical pickups continued with the C-Series of 1954 to 1956 and the Power Giant Era of 1957 to 1960. Dodge introduced its first overhead valve V-8 engines (Hemis in medium and heavy-duty trucks only), the industry's first conventional cab 4WD light-duty trucks and fully-automatic transmissions (including push-button control). Only the cab was redesigned in mid-year 1955, at which time visibility took a giant step forward with a full-width rear window and a wrap around windshield. For driver convenience and comfort, cab interiors were redesigned to make the driver's task easier and more productive.

The practical pickup's reputation continued in the Sweptline Era of 1961 to 1971 with the introduction of Dodge's economical, long running slant six engines. The second practical first for Dodge in 1961 was the alternator, an innovation quickly copied by the entire industry. A practical new type of pickup in this era was the crew cab, another Dodge first.

The Life Style Era trucks of 1972 to 1978 are the last series in our study. In 1973 Dodge announced a practical innovation which will go down as the most important innovation in all pickup history—the Club Cab, another practical idea which has since been copied by all other pickup manufacturers. A second practical innovation of this era was electronic ignition, an advancement which speaks for itself.

A 1997 Dodge truck television ad, for Rams and Dakotas, has this line in it: "Dodge trucks are honest, get the job done kind of trucks." That statement ties in wonderfully with our theme of Dodge pickups being "practical." What has made Dodge trucks practical and honest products through the years is innovative engineering. Chrysler Corporation was founded on the premise that engineers would play key roles in the operation of the Company, and for many years the Corporation was run by the "Triumvirate." This word refers to the three hand picked engineers Mr. Chrysler hired even before the Corporation officially came into being. The three, Fred Zeder, Owen Skelton and Carl Breer, were also known as the "Three Musketeers." In Walter Chrysler's own words, "These three young automotive engineers were wizards. They seemed to be the parts of a single, extraordinary engineering intelligence." Mr. Chrysler hired them in 1920 while he worked for a banking group to save the ailing Willys-Overland Company.

In the early years these men drove the company, they were totally immersed in research and development to make Chrysler number one in engineering. They succeeded admirably. To this day Chrysler retains its excellence in engineering reputation. The following story will illustrate what I mean. It begins in the mid-1930s when diesel powered heavy-duty trucks first began to make an impact on the big truck market, thanks to the pioneering work of Clessie Cummins. The Three Musketeers, always seeking to be on the cutting edge of everything new, designed and built their own diesel engine. It was offered only in three-ton trucks (Dodge's biggest model at that time), making Chrysler the only major automotive manufacturer building its own diesel engine, except for giant rival GM. One has to wonder if this was a sound business decision because, even if Dodge would have captured half of the total diesel truck business in 1939, Chrysler's diesel sales volume would not have covered engineering, testing and development costs. The truth is that the diesel was developed because it was the thing to do, not because it was an economically sound decision. Through the years Chrysler Corporation has many engineering "firsts" in trucks as well as cars to its credit.

An aftermarket slide-in canopy cover converted a VC half-ton pickup into a canopy express.

This 133-inch wheelbase one-ton pickup, model VD, featured a nine foot cargo box.

The 1940 Dodge VC half-ton pickup was powered by a 201 cubic inch (ci) L-head six cylinder.

Dodge built pickups ranging in size from one-half to one-and-one-half-tons in 1940. A three-quarter-ton VD-15 is shown here.

Dodge was the Army's preferred manufacturer for light-duty 4WD military trucks. A 1940 VC-3 closed cab pickup with civilian styling is shown. *John Zentmyer*

The second series 1941 half-ton 4WD trucks featured military styling. Shown is a WC-38 closed cab pickup.

All Dodge pickup cargo boxes in this era featured wooden floors to prevent cattle's hoofs from slipping during transport. A 1941 half-ton is shown.

During the 1940s pickups began to develop a "Jack-of-all-trades" reputation. A 1941 half-ton is shown.

Only in 1941 and 1942 did Dodge pickups have the lower horizontal chrome grille bars seen on this 1941 three-quarter-ton.

The biggest pickup Dodge built in 1941 was the one-and-one-half-ton *dually*.

Civilian half-ton pickups with painted grilles went into production early in 1945. This photo is dated March 23, 1945.

The workhorse of Dodge's 1945 pickup line was the three-quarter-ton model.

Dodge's largest post-war 2WD pickup was the 133-inch wheelbase one-ton, designated a WD-21.

This pre-production 1945 Power Wagon with combat wheels features a conventional one-ton pickup's cargo box.

The Power Wagon's styling was unchanged from 1946 to 1950. A 1946 Power Wagon with front mounted power winch is shown.

All 1946 WC half-ton pickups were produced with chrome grilles, however the chrome front bumper was not a factory standard.

The big one-ton 1947 WD-21 133-inch pickup was a big seller. Dodge also built a smaller WD-21 120-inch wheelbase one-ton pickup.

The rear view of this 1948 one-ton B-Series pickup clearly shows the improved rear and side visibility offered by its new rear-quarter windows.

The wheelbase on the new 1948 one-ton B-Series pickup was shortened to 126-inches from the 133-inches of the preceding series.

DODGE
DODGE
B-108 ½ TON EXPRESS
EQUIPPED WITH
ROCKFORD
PANEL CONVERSION

This 1948 aftermarket panel conversion allowed buyers to easily and quickly convert a half-ton pickup into a panel.

This standard cab 1948 B-1 half-ton pickup was Dodge's lowest cost pickup. The two color paint scheme was standard.

Manually operated wrecker equipment on this one-ton pickup was installed either by the dealer or a truck equipment company.

Stainless steel grille bars on light-duty B-1 trucks of 1948-1949 were standard equipment. Medium and heavy-duty trucks' grille bars were painted body color as on this 1949 half-ton pickup.

This side view of a 1949 B-Series half-ton pickup affords an excellent perspective on Dodge's high-side cargo box.

The low-side box was the new standard for 1950, the high-side became an option.

Dodge built cars and trucks in its San Leandro, CA plant in 1950. A half-ton pickup is being assembled in the foreground.

Fluid Drive equipped light-duty trucks were an industry first for Dodge in 1950. The signs on these trucks say they are equipped with Fluid Drive.

The low-side pickup cargo box was continued as standard for the 1951 B-3 Series as seen on this 1951 standard cab half-ton.

The high-side cargo box shown on this 1951 deluxe cab half-ton out sold the low-side by an enormous margin.

The low-side box was standard on three-quarter-ton pickups as well as on one-ton pickups shown on this 1951 116-inch wheelbase pickup with a seven-and-one-half-foot box.

Dodge's biggest 1951 pickup was this *dually* built on a 126-inch chassis with a nine-foot express box.

Only in 1951 was the chrome plated grille offered as an extra-cost option. This half-ton pickup with its distinctive two-tone paint scheme is a Spring Special.

Dodge management continued the B-3 Series for 1952 without styling changes. A 1952 half-ton is shown.

Dodge sold more Spring Special pickups in 1953 than any previous year. Many were equipped with the new Truck-O-Matic semi-automatic transmission.

Pontoon-style fenders were the most noticeable styling change for 1953. This truck is equipped with the Truck-O-Matic transmission as seen on a hood side name plate.

NEW!

B-116 LONG WHEEL-BASE 1/2-TON

Of the Big Three, Dodge was the first to manufacture a half-ton pickup on a long wheelbase chassis with a seven-and-one-half-foot cargo box.

The V-8 engine was new late in the 1954 model year, the first year of the C-1 Series.

This six cylinder powered 1954 half-ton pickup is a top-of-the-line model as seen by its wheel covers, two-tone paint and rear quarter cab windows.

The low-side cargo box was standard equipment in 1954 for half-ton pickups as seen on this early engineering prototype.

Three-quarter-ton pickups were a favorite with farmers because of their ability to haul heavy loads.

46

This eye catching 1954 half-ton pickup painted for display at a press preview event was called the "Polka Dot".

In 1954 all pickup manufacturers boasted of the lowest pickup loading height. The Dodge salesman is carefully explaining how low this pickup's bed is.

C-1 Series trucks carried over into 1955 without change. A deluxe 1955 half-ton pickup is shown.

Dodge engineers increased the displacement of the V-8 engine from 241 ci in 1954 to 259 ci in 1955.

C-3 Series trucks were introduced in mid-year 1955. They featured a restyled cab with a full-width rear window and wrap around windshield.

C-3 Series Dodge trucks offered two-tone paint schemes as a standard.

Note that the wooden cargo box floor shown in this 1955 three-quarter-ton pickup is painted black, which was standard procedure.

The only exterior styling change on the original Power Wagon was the cargo box with embossed sides which was new for 1951. This Power Wagon is a 1956 model.

It was on the C-3 Series trucks that Dodge engineers first offered four levels of cab trim: Standard, Deluxe, Custom (shown) and Custom Regal.

The full-width rear window may be one of the most sensible and practical improvements ever in truck cab design, seen here on a 1956 half-ton V-8 powered pickup.

In 1956 grille bars and surround were always painted Chilean Beige regardless of cab color.

The biggest pickup Dodge engineers crafted for 1957 was this monster one-ton *dually*.

This 1957 Dodge half-ton conventional cab Power Wagon represents two industry firsts: a ninety-degree opening hood and the first light-duty 4WD one-half and three-quarter-ton trucks.

Factory photos of the 1957 Sweptside D100 pickup are extremely rare.

This 1957 Dodge three-quarter-ton pickup carried a seven-and-one-half-foot cargo box.

Hooded headlights on this 1957 D100 pickup cause its front fenders to appear to sweep forward.

Truckers called this method of delivering new trucks Piggy Back. The 1957 D200 three-quarter ton pickup at the rear is being carried on the piggy backed D500 chassis cab.

Here is an example of a highly accessorized 1957 Dodge pickup. Note its chrome plated front bumper, bumper guards, grille bars and headlight surrounds.

The Sweptside D100 pickup returned for its second year in 1958, now with a restyled hood, front fenders and grille.

Conventional cab one-half and three-quarter-ton Power Wagons were new in 1957, the one-ton version was added for 1958. A Fargo is shown.

The 1959 Dodge D100 Sweptside pickup was discontinued in January 1959 when the new Sweptline wide-side pickup was introduced.

The new 1959 Dodge D300 Sweptline with a cab-wide cargo box was a very big and handsome pickup.

Early in 1959 the Dodge D100 Sweptline pickup was introduced and caused the demise of the Sweptside D100.

The U.S. Navy purchased this 1960 Dodge D300 one-ton Sweptline for its huge carrying capacity.

Dodge Truck's style leader for 1960 was this handsome D100 Sweptline pickup.

Dodge marketing named its narrow box pickup the Utiline after the wide box Sweptline was introduced in 1959.

The Sweptline D100 half-ton pickup in the all new 1961 Dodge truck line was called the Dart after the extremely popular mid-size Dodge car.

A half-ton 1961 D100 Dart pickup piggy backed to a D500 chassis cab.

Utiline models with wood floor construction continued in the Sweptline Series.

A hard working 1961 W100 half-ton Power Wagon pickup labors in an oil field.

Crew cab pickups were first offered by Dodge in the 1961 model year.

The only styling change for 1962 was an improved grille seen on this 1962 D100 half-ton Utiline pickup.

Keeping with Dodge Truck management's policy of no change for change sake, 1963 styling was unchanged from 1962.

As in 1963, there were no styling changes in 1964 models. A D200 three-quarter-ton Sweptline pickup is shown.

All new for 1964 was this practical little A100 pickup powered by either a 170 ci or 225 ci slant six engine.

Possibly the most exciting new model ever offered by Dodge up to this time was the Custom Sports Special pickup, available with up to 365 hp.

The styling which began in 1962 lasted until mid-year 1965 when Dodge pickups were extensively reengineered and restyled. A first series 1965 D100 half-ton Sweptline pickup is shown.

The second series 1965 pickup featured an all new grille and single headlights. A D200 three-quarter-ton Sweptline pickup is shown.

Second series 1965 models carried over unchanged into 1966. Shown is a one-ton Utiline pickup.

An untiring workhorse in the 1966 Dodge line was the D200 three-quarter-ton Utiline pickup.

The top-of-the-line pickup for 1967 was the Sweptline model shown featuring a textured paint cab roof, paint filled side molding, full wheel covers and white sidewall tires.

Beginning in 1962 Dodge built crew cab pickups in the assembly plant on the same line as standard cab trucks. A 1967 D200 crew cab is shown.

Front styling was freshened up for 1968 through the use of a bolder grille and smaller headlight surrounds.

Since 1961 the only crew cab pickups offered were the D200 and W200 three-quarter-ton models. A D200 is shown.

Dodge was big in camping and campers in 1968. The popular W200 Power Wagon Camper Special sold very well.

The smallest and lowest priced full-size pickup for 1969 was the D100 short-box Utiline.

The first year for the upscale Adventurer model was 1969. A D100 half-ton Sweptline Adventurer is shown.

A second top-of-the-line 1969 pickup is the D100 Adventurer with a black stipple painted cab roof and full wheel covers.

The U.S. Navy was an important customer in 1970 for the
D200 Utiline crew cab pickup.

The last year for the Sweptline Series pickups was 1971. This is a 1971 D100 Dude (a graphics package only) half-ton.

The all new reengineered and restyled Life Style Series Dodge pickups for 1972 were improved in many ways. The D100 Custom shown was the lowest priced pickup in 1972.

The upscale D100 Adventurer model was the most expensive 1972 Dodge pickup.

The 1972 D200 Adventurer Camper Special 9000 was a favorite with slide-on camper owners.

The most important new pickup cab type in all of pickup history was the 1973 Dodge Club Cab. A D200 model is shown.

The fanciest pickup sold by Dodge in 1973 was the D100 Adventurer Special Edition.

A common sight on the nation's freeways in 1973 was this D200 Camper Special 9000 with an expensive over-the-cab slide-in camper.

The 1974 D200 pickup was an All-American workhorse special.

The 1977 Dodge W200 Power Wagon was not only an attractive truck but also an extremely capable and practical truck.

When the U.S. Army purchased regular production pickups in lieu of specially engineered military trucks, they bought this 1977 M880 4WD one-and-one-quarter-ton cargo truck. *John Zentmyer collection*

Most 1977 Dodge Warlocks were painted black, but Dodge offered them in several colors including red, as this truck is painted.

The 1978 Dodge Midnight Express was a special model patterned after the Li'l Red Express and sold only in California. *Bob Bray*

One of Dodge Truck's all-time favorite collector trucks is the flashy high-performance 1978 Li'l Red Express. *Monty Montgomery*

Dodge built more pickups in model year 1978 than in any other in its history. This 1978 D150 Adventurer SE pickup is one of only 74 half-ton trucks equipped with the 440 V-8. *Monty Montgomery*

This 1978 Dodge W150 Power Wagon Custom short bed with a 440 V-8 is an extremely rare truck. *Monty Montgomery*